Dedication

I dedicate this book to parents, in particular parents of teenagers. Never stop praying for your children. God does hear your prayers. Your prayers make a difference. May God's loving hands shower your children with blessings, protection, peace and joy.

Maria A Flores

Response from a mother's prayer for her daughter:

"Treat her as a butterfly. Be kind, gentle, and loving. She seeks your attention, acceptance and love. Never forget, I loved you first. You are my beloved daughter."

This Book Belongs To:

_____

Your comfort
delights my soul
(Psalm 94:19)

Butterfly Coloring & Activity Book: Encouragement for Parents

By: Maria A Flores

Touch the Heart, Reach the Soul LLC
Polk City, FL, USA

Butterfly Coloring and Activity Book: Encouragement for Parents

2024 Copyright by Touch the Heart, Reach the Soul LLC

ONLINE BOOKSTORE, APPAREL & GIFT ITEMS:
http://touchtheheartreachthesoul.store

Scriptures are taken from the New King James Version. Copyright 1982 by Thomas Nelson. Used by permission. All rights reserved.

Manuscript, design, illustrations, and book cover by Maria A Flores

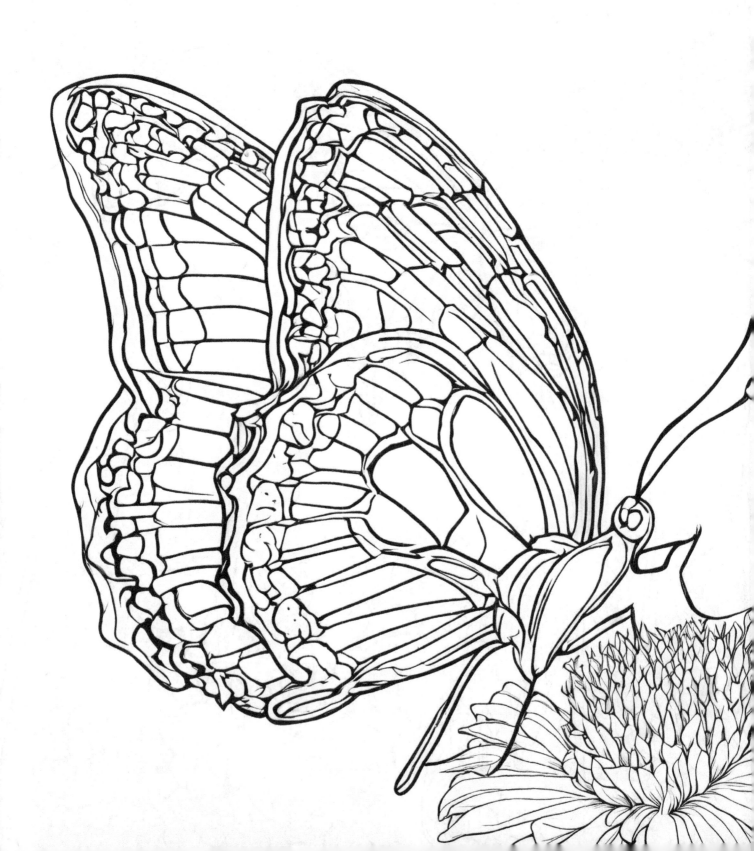

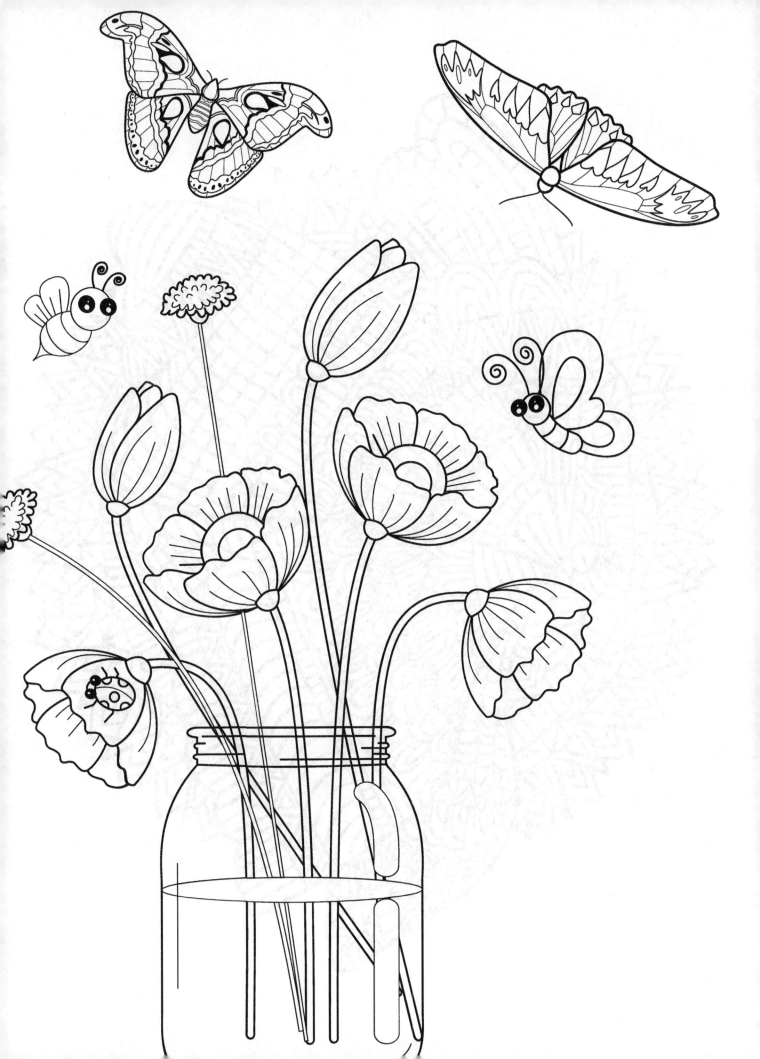

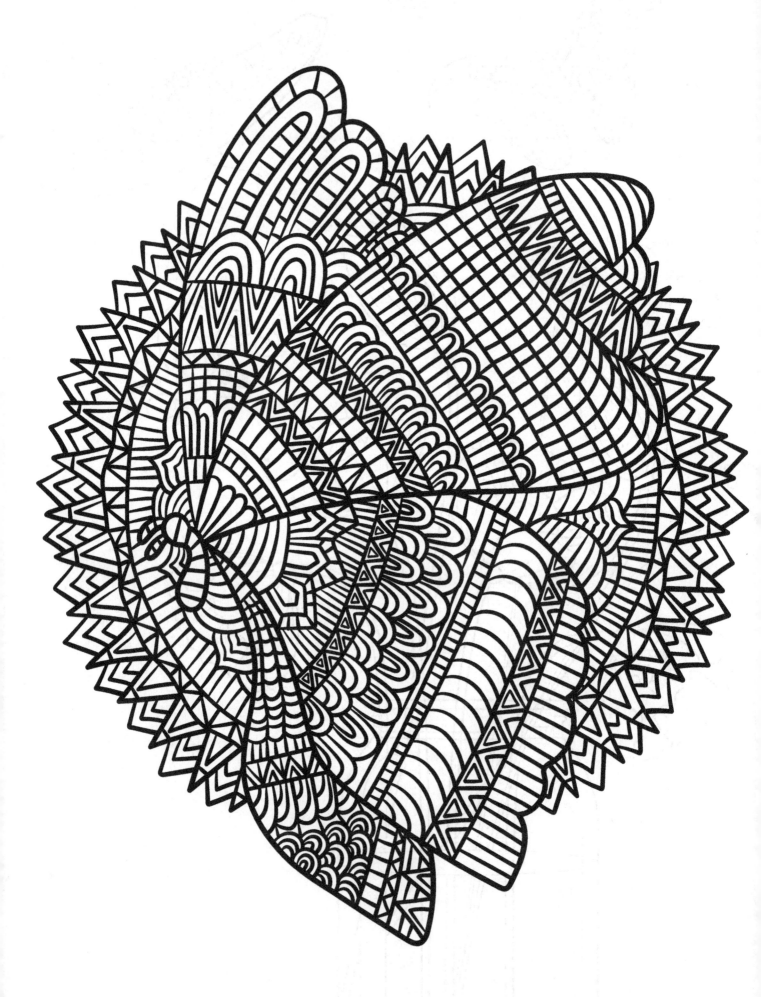

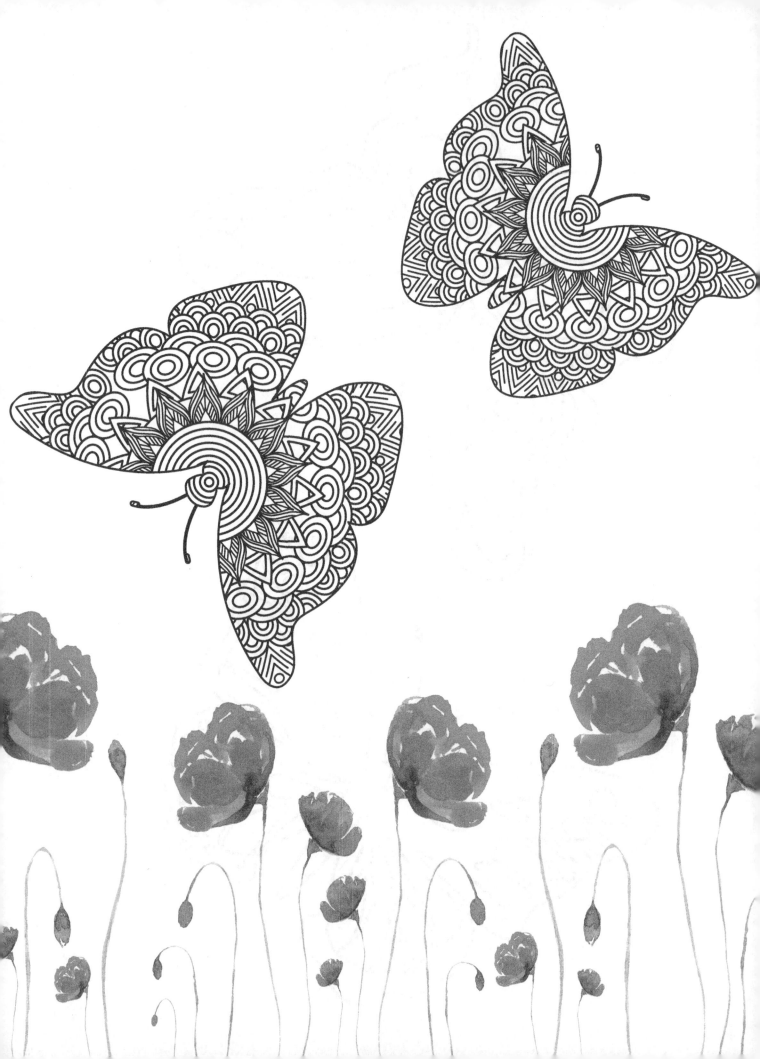

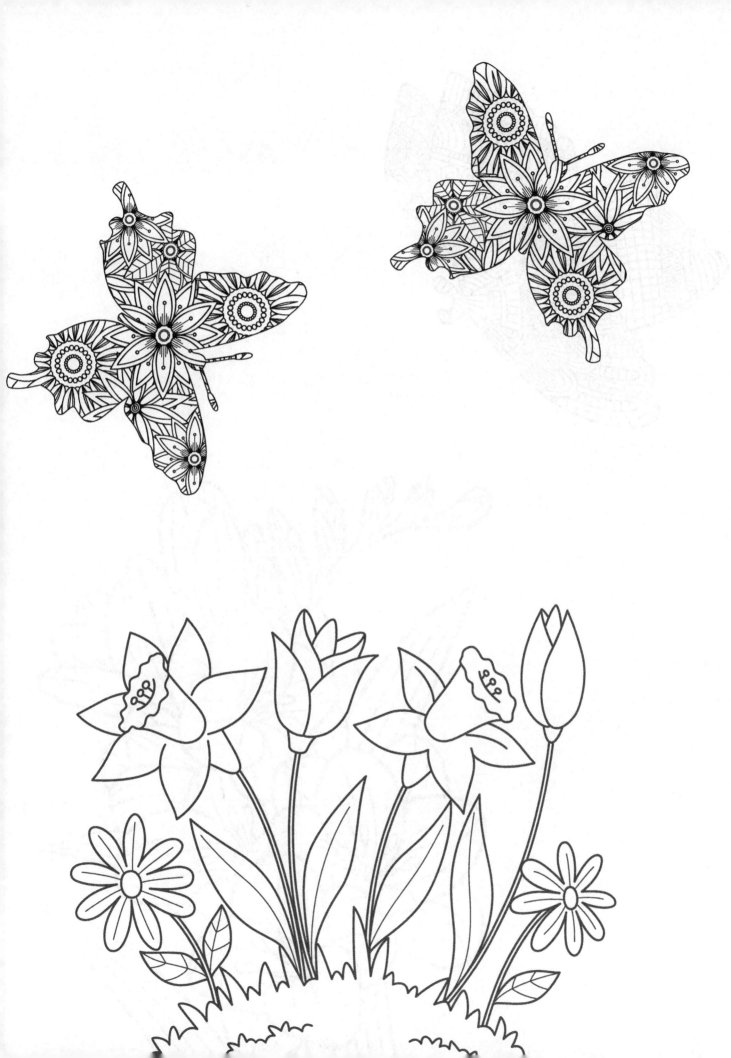

Color together!

Be still and know
that I am God.
(Psalm 46:10)

Children are the heritage of the Lord
(Psalms 127:3)

Fathers, do not provoke your children (Ephesians 6:4)

Children's children are the crown of old men
(Proverbs 17:6)

Be of good courage, and he shall strengthen your heart (Psalm 31:24)

Peace I leave with you, my peace I give to you (John 14:27)

I will fear no evil; for thou art with me (Psalm 23:4)

Just
BELIEVE

you've
GOT THIS

you are SPECIAL

Prayer Requests

Prayer Requests

Prayer Requests

Prayer Requests

Prayer Requests

Prayer Requests

Prayer Requests

Prayer Requests

Prayer Requests

Prayer Requests

If you have enjoyed this book, please write a review on Amazon.

To see a full collection of faith based books, apparel & gift items from TOUCH THE HEART, REACH THE SOUL visit us at
http://touchtheheartreachthesoul.store
Questions/Comments:
customerservice@touchtheheartreachthesoul.com

Made in the USA
Middletown, DE
03 September 2024

60017191R00071